This Book Is De
To My Wife, Is ....

Oh, blushing, vestal, tender heart
Thy bloom of youth is now depart
Your calm perfection now imparts
Serenity, in a timeless art.

Contents:

Section 1

Love and Desire

Page/Title:

Section 2

A Wandering Mind

Page/Title:

Section 3

We're Not Happy About This!

Page/Title:

Section 4

Oh, What a Life

Page/Title:

Section 5

It's a Uniformed Life

Page/Title:

Section 6

The Dark Side of Life

Page/Title:

Section 7

Nature Has The Last Word

Page/Title:

Introduction:

Throughout my life, I have often found myself thinking in a rhyming, rhythmic, poetic beat; usually during a period of extreme, emotional stress.

It wasn't until 2004 that I felt the urge to actually write a poem.

The catalyst for that had been the first death I had ever witnessed – that of my father; ending his brave battle with cancers.

Fortunately, I have had very few 'stress-write' situations since. (I am now content to write whenever the pleasant urge takes hold).

So why this book of my poems, and why now?

Well, when I wrote 'A Ripple on the Gene Pool', recently, (see page 27) I began to wonder about what I could leave behind - apart from the genes in my offspring - which might last a while longer than my dust and vague memories of me.

And this is the result - my first book - my gift to prosperity - and you now hold a copy of it! (Don't you just love an inflated ego?).

It is now late March in 2021, so how am I doing? Is it lasting?

I hope you enjoy my efforts, but, whether you love them or loathe them, please don't destroy the book – just pass it on. ☺

Best wishes,
Colin Clark
1950 - Whenever.

Section 1
Love and Desire

Thought for the day.

Even in love, some things are best kept secret.
But then, .love is often the death of reason.

Just One Glimpse

I first saw her in nineteen sixty-four,
As she glided, across our classroom floor.
At first, I caught a fleeting glimpse,
But I sensed I wanted more.

And then, got a side view,
It nearly knocked me flat.
I remember thinking, crassly,
'I must have some of that!'

Across the desks, I sent a note,
Requesting our first date.
She'd captured me so swiftly,
As I'm sure some can relate.

We dated for a year or so.
Nothing serious, you understand
But, at the tender age of fourteen,
Who knows where the cards will land?

We parted for three lonely years,
Each singing to different bands
But, if we ever thought, 'It's over.'
Soon, Cupid played his hand:

I met her brother in the street.
He said, 'She still thinks you're sweet.'
So I wrote a quick, short letter, and,
Oh, boy, did our hearts beat!

We married that October,
In nineteen sixty-eight.
My father drove me to the church.
Hours early, in case we were late.

I stood, real close beside her;
Swore devotion to the end
Even now we're standing closely,
Our shadows continue to blend.

Now, we're in our 53rd year -
A journey of laughter and tears.
There could never be someone better,
To travel with through those years.

Now surrounded by our family,
Each, a gift of the gods;
The result of one short glimpse in school.
I wonder, what were the odds?

You Make My Day

I come down every morning
To see love in your eyes.
Your happiness, so visible
I take a contented sigh.

You point to a hot beverage
Then you turn toward the stove.
I drop into an empty seat
As my mind begins to roam.

Another workday has started
With much to task my brain
But then you turn to grace me
With that loving smile again.

So, nothing will mar my happiness
No matter what folks say
As I toil and slave; remembering
That you have made my day!

That Smile

That smile, as you wave through the window
You may think just sends me away
But I promise, my sweet little darling
It stays with me all through the day.

Your twinkling blue eyes simply blind me.
The warmth you emit warms my soul.
I can't wait 'til I get home each night
You make life perfect and whole.

For many years we have battled
The world and the angst it can bring.
But, nothing can beat our devotion.
We are armoured against everything.

We have been like soldiers together
A fantastic love to defend
No matter what they next throw us
We will win. We'll fight to the end.

A Perfect Start to the Day

Well, I went to bed at something past then
Re-awoke once or twice, though I know not quite
when
But, when I finally 'woke, I'd a moment of Zen;
I thought, 'It's Sunday now'. So I lay down again.

But then, in my dreams, I had a nice thought
That it's moments like these, which cannot be bought
When our wants and needs should never be fought
And in that dreamlike state, I knew what I sought.

Then, in came my wife; I knew what she'd see
She's my hearts' desire; so, I knew she'd please me.
With a loving smile, she stroked my knee
Said, 'I know what you need; here's a nice cup of tea.'

.Why Do I Say...

Why do I say, I love you
When you say, you already know?
I want them to be my last words to you;
If someday, I can't come home.

Why do I stare into your eyes,
When it makes my poor heart-rate soar?
I see, in their depths, perfection
So, I tremble to my very core.

Why do I never say goodbye
When we part, each day, at our door?
I don't want our love conversation to end;
I want to talk more and more.

So, I'll tell you this every morning.
I'll whisper it; then I'll roar,
'I love you! I'll love you, my sweetheart!'
For as long as I dance on life's floor.

And if, some day, my heart implodes
Or my mind reaches foreign shores
Please remember these simple words, my dear,
"I will love you forever more."

The Truth of You

Whether green
Or blushing blue
Your eyes reveal
The truth of you

Neither tears
Nor paint disguise
Can ever hide
What's in the eyes

And while life
May take its toll
Eyes reflect
Your very soul

You

No verse could hold the words
To describe my love for you.
No painting has the colours
That illustrate my view.

No dream creates a better world
Than the one I share with you.
No wonder I'm so dizzy
At the very thought of you.

She

She might not say it often
But I see it every day
In the thousand ways she shows her love
They mean more than words convey

Her touch, her smile, that kiss, that hug
Are the icing on lifes' cake
Who knows where I would be today;
Because, without her, I would break

She is the very heart of me
The soul I can't define
She is the very best of me
I thank God she is mine

Love is in the Eyes

When the lust and wonder of the honeymoon
Waxes and wanes with the phase of the moon
When reality slaps you, all too soon
Dragging you, screaming from the love bedroom

As those sexy whispers in your ear
Morph into snores or tantrums and tears
Replacing 'Yes. Yes' with, 'Not tonight Dear.'
You've entered the real world, I fear.

Once endearing traits, now seem, just strange
And their big ideas sound quite deranged
When you desperately pray for something to change
When you wish for a button to pause/re-arrange!

But what of your old dreams, where have they all gone
Have they flown to the heavens; to Icarus' sun?
Or are they just lying dormant, waiting to be done?
Is it time to decide; should you stay, or just run?

But remember that girl; you saw that first day
Or the boy, you adored and prayed they'd say
Those magic words of 'Please. Please stay.'
Now, where did they go; did they all fly away?

So, look at your partner. Look into their eyes
There is your history; the lows and the highs.
If they're loving eyes, they will tell you no lies.
So open your arms, and both of you; fly!

Wrinkled Eyes and Wrinkled Thighs

Between us, wrinkled eyes
give lie to our tears
as if passing years
are the reason we cry

How wrong they be
those who cannot see
these are tears of happiness
springing from our ancient guise.

And these wrinkled thighs give lie
to those hours of impassioned cries
as we made children such as these;
who dance through life so free.

Oh, that we could go back
to those wild days and nights
of rawness, heat and passion,
but then, if indeed, we could;
we'd not be sitting here now?

Hidden Desires

What sets me afire
Are my hidden desires
And my lust for a girl who's not free
But I can't keep these thoughts
Inside of my head
No matter how quiet I be.

When she is close by
My brain starts to fry
While my heart beats way out of tune
But no-one must know
Though I dread it will show
While that girl is my fathers' new queen!

Love and Kisses

I've breathed warm sweet whispers into ears small and
neat;
Survived the collision of lips on hard teeth
I've failed that French sliding of cheek next to cheek;
And met sniggers while kissing their hands soft and
sleek
But still, all my hopes of real kisses are bleak
Perhaps it comes down to my lack of technique.

But now, while my time here is fast running down
Still, all of the ladies just turn, shrug and frown.
None of them want to see me hanging 'round
I guess, all they see is a silly old clown.
If I cannot find love here and soon settle down
I think it is best if I simply left town.

But, where does one go to find true happiness
When everyone 'round me is having success
Do I place a sad ad in the popular press
Or climb up high mountains, just to impress?
My life now just seems such a horrible mess
When all that I seek is a lovers caress.

My Mum tried to tell me where I'm going wrong;
"In your quest to find love, you may come on too strong.
If you learned just one dance, or maybe a song,
Or even a joke; that should help things along.
If you make the girls smile, you just cannot go wrong.
Love's not a game. but it must be played long."

I know I should act on the things that she said
Though the thought of rejection still fills me with dread
With the things that are spinning around in my head
I'm tempted to give up and just curl up in bed.
But my need is too strong, so I'm forging ahead
One day, I'll find love. One day, I will wed!

Coming Home

The room I inhabit is crowded,
but I don't see a single soul,
because the place I am in is my comfort zone;
it contains only you alone.

The distance between us is massive,
but our hearts are as close as can be,
I can feel your warmth and your heartbeat;
you are all that matters to me.

I simply adore you my darling,
I have spent too much time out here,
This uniform has its demands I know,
but the end is now drawing near.

We've been fighting for freedom and liberty
for the people of Afghanistan,
So they may lead their lives terror free
and each is a truly free man.

And now my last tour is over;
I have just a few hours to go,
I'll soon be back in your arms again
and this time it's not a furlough.

I join my flight in the morning.
I've checked all the days off on my chart.
I can hardly wait to be with you again,
when tomorrow becomes our new start.

We'll Be Together Again

I miss you my darling, the light of my life.
I search for you each night, in winters moonlight.
But, I know when these sad tears have finally dried.
How soon I'll be standing there, right by your side.

Please, know I still love you, oh, so tenderly,
Although your earth spirit has now been set free.
Each night I have whispered, sweet words to your face,
My mind shuffling pictures, I'll never erase.

Though my light is hidden, 'neath dark, stormy clouds,
My heart is now beating, thunderously loud.
When I see you next, I'll be totally free,
Then we'll be together, for eternity.

My body is trembling, my darling best friend.
It knows we'll be meeting, before this nights end.
I love you my sweetheart, but don't shed a tear,
I'm coming right now, for that moment is here.

Bang! Bang!

His Silent Scream

I scream in the morning, I scream throughout the night.
I scream when alone and I scream as I write.
But, my screams are not heard, for silent they be;
I cannot shout out, in case others hear me.

My scream is for love, for your warmth, for your
touch.
I scream from my heart, I need you so much.
As we sit together, though light-years apart,
I yearned for your body, your heat, and your heart.

So long I have shouted; at what cupid has done.
The life we could have, the laughter, the fun.
I must have done wrong, in another life, past.
But now you have wed, the die has been cast.

I wish I could leave this party with you,
But that's just a dream; I've more penance to do.
It's no use me wishing, I know it just hurts.
I must really deserve to bear this great curse.

It seems to have lasted, a century or two,
'Though my chance is over, I really need you.
I'm hurting. I'm aching. I'm twisted inside,
It's your choice in love; I cannot abide.

So now it's out loud - my howl at the moon,
But if you want to join me, please make it soon.
I'll wait until morning; praying through the night,
That you'll get this message. Make everything right,

Be You

From an oasis to deserts of blistering sand.
From love to rejection and hate.
That's where over-bending; in trying to please,
Goes the man who realises too late.

When you act like a puppy and whine for a touch.
When you roll so your belly is bare,
When respect for yourself has flown out the door,
Be sure that no-one will care.

She won't want the 'you', that you'll turn out to be,
She won't want a sham or a fake.
You'll be neither the man she married you for,
nor the one that you thought you would make.

The way to win through is to stay true to you,
To the man that she saw that first day.
'Cos when you alter and bend too much, in the end,
The real you is left by the way.

So ignore my advice at your peril.
Heed these words for every-ones sake.
Stand up and be strong,
Tho' you may oft be wrong.
Learn these lessons before it's too late.

Wake up to the perils of niceness.
Beware of the cost of being good.
Be the man that she knew,
And she'll be true to you,
Or you'll wake up in solitude!

Message in a Bottle

I was cast off by my first love, after just one fleeting
kiss.
But, nothing could prepare me for this grievous abyss.
Unwanted and tossed wildly, on oceans just like this.
I'm bruised and feel rejected by the only one I miss.

I drift around aimlessly, across these barren seas.
Confused by her actions and what she needs
Does she look for a lover with strong arms to squeeze?
Alas, it's now obvious, that cannot be me.

Though, I could live for a hundred years
I'd never see clearly through these salty tears.
Though some days are better when dense fogs clear
I still cannot cope with these constant fears.

A passing friend told me: one of the few,
I have much good news, but sadly, none of you'.
He warned me to stay out here, out on the blue,
Because danger awaited. I hadn't got a clue.

The world seems against me. But what is my crime?
I just want to live in a happier clime.
I've a hand-written message, out here on the brine.
But, will I ever get to deliver it sometime?

It seems; no-one wants me in their universe.
and very country thinks; I'm a curse.
They want to destroy me, by fire or worse.
I'm so undeserving, it's utterly perverse!

 I can't understand the words she said to me
When she tearfully tossed me into this barren sea.
If she loves another, who could that be
When her kiss said she loved me, before she cast me
free!

So, with this in my heart, it's here I must remain
Never seeking landfall; to never love again.
Though all this has hurt me, I really can't complain
I'm just a plastic bottle, tossing in the rain.

Poor You

Time should distance us from the past
Bad memories should simply struggle to last
But now and then, against our will
The worst of them holds fast, still

So, while age may have cooled her passions
Your emotions might still be the same
One smile will fan smouldering embers
Into wild, hot, roaring flames

Her beauty and shape may have faded
While the love in your heart may still grow
But, there's not very much you can do, my friend
And this you already know.

But you'll keep right on, persisting
Ignoring everyone's advice;
She turned her back and went walking
Said. You're not worth the sacrifice'.

But, you still won't stop. You idiot
You stand in the corner and cry
You continue to send silly messages
Knowing she'll never reply.
Poor you.

A Salute to Our Friendship

I bow to our long friendship, my level-headed friends.
You've always stood beside me, and rarely condescend.
I'm often in the wrong, but you've been there to defend,
So, when I say and do the wrong things, I don't mean to offend.

Yes, you've always been there for me; on you I can depend
Though, how I earned that friendship, I'll never comprehend.
You've kept me out of trouble, so now I must extend
My thanks for all your loyalty; I will love you to the end.

Dear Friend

Today I sat and counted all
The friends I've loved and knew.
Of those who meant the most to me,
The first in line was you.

Then thinking back the other way,
I asked if I could say,
Which friends could I depend on, if
My own life went astray?

At first, the answer puzzled me.
How could I be alone?
When I've hundreds waiting close to hand,
In my cherished mobile phone.

And then I thought. 'How silly!'
There really is no doubt. For,
While most would only read my words,
It's you who'd hear my shout.

So I wanted just to thank you
For being such a friend. And
to pledge the very warmest love;
Devotion to the end.

So, when all the world's against you, and
you're feeling down some day.
Forget the time, just tap my name,
I'm just a call away.

Section 2

A Wandering Mind

Thought for the day.

Never insist that something is 'idiot-proof,
because new designs are invented every day
.

A Ripple on the Gene Pool

What will be your legacy,
What will you leave behind;
Just a ripple on the gene pool,
Is that all they will find?

You could tell all those who follow
That you had a creative mind, and
You've left them something tangible;
A product of that mind.

Show them that you lived and loved,
Much more than natures design
That you had another purpose;
Not just to propagate mankind.

But, none of that will happen
If you haven't tried to find
A use for that creative spark;
We all have, deep inside.

It needn't be too wondrous.
Nothing too refined.
Compose a poem or write some words
Whatever. You decide.

You might even paint a picture
Though your thoughts are not confined
Just use your imagination
 'Seek and you shall find'!

One day, someone will see your work
And even if unsigned
They'll know you lived before you died.
So, what will you leave behind?

Gentlemen – A Word in your Ears

If you sprinkle when you tinkle
Don't just wipe the seat.
It might be something serious
So, a doctor you should meet.

He might not seem a gentleman
('Though your butt might have a treat)
You're the only one embarrassed
He does this every week.

It's likely you won't feel much.
So, just face it with a smile.
All we who've also been there
Felt like running a mile.

But when 'prostate' starts complaining
Making peeing such a bitch.
Will your loved ones be complaining,
If you die and make them rich?

A Good Morning?

Does your alarm sing as it bids you, 'Good day?'
Or jangle each nerve as you scream, 'Go away!'

Do you stretch for a while; meet the day with a smile
Or is it; 'wrong side of bed with a mouth full of bile

Do you relax quite calmly with coffee you can taste
Or just dash off to work, on an inch of toothpaste

Do you start your day, all smiley and eager
Or with a dark frown, defeated and beleaguered

Do you take gentle swerves, on biometric curves
Or battle with your nerves, draining all reserves

Do you ensure you climb, with your ducks all in a line
Or do you view any change as an ominous sign

Do you act like a winner even when you might lose
Or is life a disaster, best cured with lots of booze

Do you view every new step as a positive change
Or maybe you're just past it. It must be your age!

Every Second Counts

Clocks tick
pendulums swing
no control
over anything

Time moves on
move along
'til the clock stops
then you're gone

That's your lot
time to trot
little left
when corpses rot

Had your fun
no-one won
can't turn back
you're done

Gone today
making way
Then a fresh lot
will have their say

Memories fade
then decay
recycled again
another day

Nothing lasts
once we've passed
nothing stands
except the past.

So make the best
As you've been blessed
With another day
So sod the rest!

Enjoy every second, because
Time doesn't pass – we do.

Morning Glory

If you get up very early
And face towards the east
You'll start your working day
With a veritable feast.

Just before the sun comes up
When all is hushed and quiet,
A false dawn will greet us and
Prepare us for the riot.

There's a twittering of birds all around,
But soon they turn that way
In silence; like they're telling us,
They've nothing more to say.

But, hold your breath, and wait awhile
What's past was just foreplay
Remember this, 'between time',
Throughout your busy day.

Because, all at once, Dawns Chorus starts
The din assaults our ears,
All birds let loose with ribald hearts,
As they call out to their peers.

'Wake up! Wake up!', they cry and shout.
'A new day has just begun.'
'Wake up, my lazy feathered friends.,
Come on, join in the fun!'

And soon men slowly stir themselves;
With sleep still in their eyes,
They wash before they dress for toil
In every type of guise.

They zombie march off to their work;
To win life's glorious fights.
But, they'll have missed the beauty
'Twix the darkness and the light.

In-Between Times

It's that time after eating
That wonderful meal;
Sat back in your chair,
Now, how did that feel?

Did you let out your belt
for an easier fit
before calling for the bill
and paying for it?

Did you,
Look to your partner
Share a smile,
Pause for a moment
Wait a while?

That's an 'In-between time';
That lull between acts.
That priceless moment which
Oft' fall through the cracks.

Like when you grab that first drink
At the end of the day
When you've had that first mouthful;
There's nothing to say.

Slowly downing your glass
Then smacking your lips
Whatever comes next
There is nothing like this.

And when you flop on your back
After losing your head
In the hot, frantic world of passion
When the 'short death' arrives
And you must close your eyes,
As sleep demands its ration

It's those golden times; between 'fight and flight'
Between battle, rest and respite.
Those dreamy, satisfying moments
Afore dreamland claims your night.

Heaven or Hell

With all the goddamned misery
Throughout our world today
I wonder what our creator
Would really have to say

Might he point at our fragilities;
Say we must kneel down and pray
Or suggest, 'Just love our neighbour
And get on with your days'?

Would he look upon us kindly
Or turn his back in disgust
Would he hit 'delete' on all of us
And turn us all to dust?

Do you dream of a place in Paradise
When your time is up, down here
Do you think you've earned a 'Well done',
When it's time to disappear?

Or is it Hell you really covet
Where the Devil feeds his spawn
Are you a Stalker in the shadows
Or a Lark who brings in the dawn?

Sh...

What is that thing which screams and shouts,
Or can whisper in your ear,
And when wielded by a loved one,
Can make hours seem like years?

What can sound quite deafening
In an empty room at night,
But when broken with good purpose,
Can make all our lives shine bright?

What is this magic weapon
Which makes big, grown men despair;
Crushing all resistance
While thickening the air?

I'll leave you for a moment
To let you figure it out.
They say it's sometimes golden
But, really, it's a verbal drought.

Time

It's a forced march
Which never marks time
Won't pause for a break
Can't stop on a dime.

It never looks back
Nor alters its pace
It just presses on
At a regular pace.

It won't glace around
It never looks down
It's all we can do
To keep feet on the ground.

Irregardless of load
It will travel its road
Whatever we're carrying
No mercy is showed

Though never eventless
The pace is relentless
'Cos we all have that date
And we can never be late!

Mirrors

You've been at those mirrors since early morn.
And I wonder, 'What do you see?'
How many more colours will you put on,
Is there someone you'd rather be?

I watch you adorn that delicate form;
A performing I get for free.
But, you seem to be fighting a new Desert Storm
Trying to hide that, 'teenage', acne!

But, that shiny-faced lass has gone out to grass.
Which you were when I first met thee.
I think it's is time to end this great farce
After all, you're now sixty-three!

We should now be there, at that family affair.
So, it really is time to flee.
I've delayed the taxi so many times,
Now they are offering the next one for free!

But still, it goes on; that same old song
While you curse like a tired old banshee.
I'm falling asleep, collapsed in a heap,
And my dreams are of breaking free

If I had a dollar, for every grim hour,
I've waited, on this settee.
I'd not be this sour if I had the power,
To fly off and live in Paree'!

Dangerous Liaisons

Silver moon-light, open window,
Curtains fluttering in the breeze.
Silken hair being combed so slowly
Mirrored eyes so gently tease.

Swanlike neck now tilting backward,
Tresses tumbling down her back.
Silken skin on slender shoulders;
No defence from loves attack.

Gentle fingers trace her forehead,
Questing kisses seek her mouth
Trembling lips are quickly parted
Good intentions soon in doubt.

Panting breaths now joined in passion
Torsos clash in wild embrace.
Bodies clasped, untamed abandon,
All pretensions losing grace.

Trembling thighs now pressing forward,
Inhibitions finally lost.
Rapid breathing, rhythmic squeezing,
No-one cares about the cost.

Then the door comes crashing inward,
Freezing all in time and space.
Two swift shots, then one soon after;
Three still bodies rest in place.

As we leave this silent picture
Please reflect on what is done.
Some liaisons last forever,
Some are ended with a gun.

I Drove Past a School Today

Darkly clad kids, waiting outside their school;
Most of them dancing, like demented fools.
Jackets wide open, trying to look 'cool'
With Rudolph red noses, dripping drool.

The other day, they seemed quite pleased
Flamingo legs and knobbly knees
Sweated, seeking, the gentlest breeze.
But, now wrapped up, in this sudden freeze.

I wonder what they'll do when they go inside;
Will they quietly listen or try to hide?
How many lessons will they abide
And how many teachers will they deride?

They know so little, but they should know,
That tutors only sow so that they might grow.
But, if all the kids just jibe to-and-fro
They will learn even less, then down they'll go.

A life of hardship waits for each one.
Party-time ends, when the schooling is done..
No job; no prospects; no cash - no fun.
It's a workers market kids, with a starting gun.

I wish I could warn them, of what's in store,
Before they tumble gaily, out of that door,
I might save one, from the jobless corps,
But, alas, I'd be seen as an ancient bore.

Good luck dear children, and fare-thee-well;
Real life kicks off at that final bell.
Don't become, a ne'er do well;
Have a worthy dream, and get caught in its spell.

Sunday

What does Sunday mean to you
Is it just another day;
A time to rest your laurels,
Or to worship God and pray?

Does 'Lords Day' mean a thing to you?
Do you have another God?
Or, does science tell the truth of things?
Are religions all a fraud?

Does it matter what I think
I am happy; go your way.
Please don't try converting me
Let's both just enjoy our day.

Had His Chips

Old Ted; tried to deceive us
He called himself a King.
But now he lays before me
Unable to command a thing.

His sockets are now empty
Though he never really saw
When I took my pointed knife to him;
and flipped his eyes onto the floor.

I took the sharpened blade;
flayed his skin into thin strips.
Though I don't believe he felt much
Though he sweated quite a bit.

I cut him into pieces;
As thin as thin could be
then dropped him into boiling fat
and had him for my tea!

(King Edwards Potatoes; ideal for chips

Not Quite What I Expected

At least I came home, my love
There's no need for that look!
I'm actually early.
You'd think I was a crook.

The boys are still partying.
I left most behind.
I only brought five home.
Please, don't be unkind.

I don't do it often.
Well, not every night.
Just show me some loving.
It will be alright.

They'll leave in just a few hours.
Yes, I'll sleep on the floor.
No, don't be so cruel, babe.
Please, don't open that door.

Oh! Whose clothes are they, sweetheart
Out there, in the yard?
They're all covered in ketchup
And some look quite charred.

And what's with that stereo
It seems it's had a smash?
You took a, what, to it
And gave it a bash?

I think you're forgetting
I'm the man of this house!
Ouch! Yes, I can hear you.
I am a blood-sucking louse.

May I have a blanket?
It's freezing out here.
The dog house is full.
Yes, I am sorry, my dear.

The Kitchen

It's a terrible place, where all must endure,
Inevitable death, by medieval torture.
Once they arrive, whether dead or alive,
They'll all leave it as corpses; for sure.

They will be carved, chopped or slashed,
Whipped, beaten, or mashed,
Boiled alive, or hung bleeding, for days.

But, no-one will care,
For dead eyes which stare,
Or the spatchcocked indignity
Of corpses laid bare.
They'll just slaver and slurp,
Consume, swallow and burp,
As they dine
On this restaurants' fine fare.

They will keep coming here,
To this gourmet frontier,
As long as Chefs keeps inventing
New dishes each year.

But never forget,
The anguish that's met,
In the kitchen -
Even onions have tears.

Silent Whispers

I'm in the darkness of your mind
That shimmer of light behind
In doubt times, I shine bright
I am the urge to do things right
      I'm always here; just out of sight

Unlike frost on winters glass
Or lingering dew on morning grass
Or wisps of mist on distant hills
They drift and fade; I never will.
      I remain. I am here still.

I'm all around and in between
Though never, really, clearly seen
I'm in your every judgmental glance,
When I step forward, you advance
      Together, we will dance.

I'm in the shadows on the wall
Always there, when spirits fall
I'm the haunting night owl call
I'm always watching, but best of all
      I will catch you when you fall

So, feel my presence.
Know and feed me.
Listen; I will set you free.
But most of all, believe in me.
      I am your conscience. I am thee.

Section 3

We're Not Happy About This!

Thought for the day

People don't, naturally, have power over us,
We allow, or give them that power.

When They Come of Age
(With All That Rage)

Life is not perfect, but have no fear;
A new harvest is coming; it does every year.
A crop of new teenagers will suddenly appear
(But, gone are those babies, we've all loved to rear).

Soon, we'll hear tantrums,
Slammed doors and wild screams.
When the real world comes crashing
Into their dreams.

After years of them watching,
On their hand-held screens
They've suddenly discovered;
Life's not how it seemed.

They have hidden in their enclaves -
Rooms hit by dirty bombs -
Minds confused by their hormones;
Bewildered by social norms.

They'll send out wise messages,
Written with great aplomb;
They'll all have it figured out
They'll know where we've gone wrong!

And then washed bodies from twisted sheets,
And with clean socks on dirty feet;
They'll emerge with educations miraculously
complete,
To parade up and down our busy streets;
Marching to a new-found beat,
While demanding their place in the driving seat.
....
Well, that position can be bittersweet.
Especially, when all one can do is bleat.
And, before you teenagers deem us old ones obsolete,
We'd all be happy, for once, to take a back seat,
In fact, we'd retire, right now, in a single heartbeat,
But, someone has to work, so the idle can eat!

The Song of Youth

That wondrous song of youth;
So often so sweetly sung
When intoned by the ignorant,
When they are all so fresh and young.

But, soon imbruing high preachers
Will re-write the verses by night.
To be imbued, wholemeal, each morning
By new listeners and old acolytes.

It's a fact that some facts are written.
But, most rumour is passed by voice.
Where they're soon accepted as gospel;
As if there's no other choice.

We know, tales distort each telling
Especially, when wisdom's ignored.
They're revered by the dim and entitled.
While disdained by the sensible horde.

Now, most will wise up, as they grow up,
As they march toward tumbleweed years.
They soon become far more enlightened,
As the fog of their youth starts to clear.

But still, there will be far too many
Who'll continue to sing those old songs.
Each verse begins with the same idle thought:
'I am right, and will never be wrong!'

So, today you will find some in politics;
They repeat their chantings, in tongues.
They continue to spout toxic nonsense;
Still poisoning the minds of our young.

Loosen the Reins!

Why do some parents never realise
We are not clones of them, in some modern disguise
Though they nurtured us through our early lives
All we want them to do now, is love and advise.

Though we still hold them all in the highest esteem
We must walk alone now, to new pastures green
Though our choices, so often, are shabbily seen
We cannot; we must not, live their faded dreams

An apple will always fall from the tree
But it's not the fruits fault when it's time to break free
We must find our own path. We don't need to agree
But, we need to find out who we want to be.

Things will never quite be just how they wished
We all have failed hopes, much to our great anguish
If they hear disagreement, we're not being childish.
We have much to accomplish; we are not so time rich.

Though we'll all love our parents, right up to the end
Too much criticism tends to offend.
They must trust us now - and right in the end
and we need them to be loving, hand-holding friends.

A Teenagers Plight

My life is all over, I really am dead,
There are things uncontrollably swamping my head.
My new life is awkward; my love-life is shit,
I want to curl up now, and die for a bit
I feel so alone.

My boss wants me 'full time' and college does too,
But how can that work, without splitting in two?
Who out there can help me; does anyone care?
You seem to float past like I'm not really there.
Please, see my pain.

Please help me and guide me out of this great mess,
but please handle gently; I'm weak with distress.
Who out there can help and show me the way,
To take back those words, I am sorry to say,
were mine?

The People Protest

While the persuasive, popular press
Publishes puerile, PC pish
Only preoccupied, primitive people
believe every word they dish

When the partisan, political powers
Present powerful points of view,
Their private, predispositions
Remain hidden from me and you.

As professional, prominent people
Preach, punctilious, unproven 'facts'
We can see self-glorification
In every scene they enact.

Where a persistently pushed proletariat
Has been pummelled by 'powers that be'
They arise; protest, then they punish
Until plasma pours out to the sea!

Propagandists, take care what you tell us.
Politicians, just watch what you do.
And publicist, give us just 'actual' facts
Because we've just enough out of you!

The Politicians Deal

Renounce your hearts
You childish upstarts
Come to heel
And accept our deal

You know we are right
Our way is the light
Relieve all your pains
Let us take the reins;

Yes, sign right here
On the dotted line.
Oh, it's too late for tears,
Now your souls are now mine!

How Many Children?

Weapons of Mass Destruction – WMD's
Carried by the people in The Land of the Free
How many corpses do they really need to see,
Before a drastic change, by official decree?

How many children should lose their lives,
Terrified senseless, as they run and hide,
As another youth hunts them, with legal carbides,
Before partisan interests are kicked aside?

Just who employs the government, over there,
When ordinary people have to run so scared?
Is it money that prevents, anti-gun being declared?
Imagine what they'd do, if they really did care.

Excommunicated

I'm feeling dejected
After being rejected
From a friendship; infected
By those I once knew

I never suspected
That I'd be elected
To be disconnected
From my best friends crew

So, now I'm neglected
I've been deselected
Though not unaffected
I know I'll fight through

A Haters Lament

I didn't relate
No love, just hate.
I'd always fight
If they took my bait.

I knew the lot
Didn't care a sot
My life was mine.
To hell with you lot!

My advice was my own.
I sat all alone.
My own shining light
On my personal throne.

But now it's a stool.
And I'm dining on gruel.
Still sitting alone
An ageing fool.

I'm yearning now.
And, I'm learning how.
But it's far too late
Anyhow.

I'd love to just prance
To life's merry dance
To have many friends
But, now there's no chance.

I'd right all my wrongs
I'd sing happy songs
I'd make many friends
To carry me on.

But the good ones all know
Just to pass by my door.
Which brings all my woes
Right to the fore

So, I deserve my lot
But for you, it's not
Too late to give
Your life its best shot.

Learn something from me
So that you can be
The best version of you
That you can possibly be.

Good luck, my lost friend
(Ok. Let's pretend)
If you work hard at life
It should come out right,
in the end, maybe.

Once, Too Often

I once had a job that fulfilled me
It kept the bad wolf from the door.
I once gave my life to the company,
Too much, for my wife, that's for sure.

Because, once I got older, they fired me.
It completely ruined our life.
For once, with no money, we argued.
Disagreements and fights became rife.

We once had a marriage to envy.
It gave succour, to us, without strife.
But once I lost heart, she soon left me.
She simply walked out of my life.

So, once my two loves had divorced me,
I lost all my passion for life.
And once I came home to this empty house,
I felt I'd been slashed with a knife.

Where once there was hope, there is silence;
Now no-one will answer the phone.
They once gave contentment and kindness.
Now, I can't face this life on my own.

I once felt such warmth; now it's winter.
There's a huge lump of ice in my chest.
Where once there was light there is darkness.
Now it's time to put this life to rest.

I once saw everything clearly.
But now I see nothing but dread.
So, once I have written these final words,
I am taking this gun to my head.

....

But, once I came too, my eyes focused
On the gun which was still in my hand.
And once I remembered my written words,
I pushed back, in horror, to stand.

All at once, I was conscious of laughter;
Happy children at play near my door
And at once, with that, the sun flooded in
And I realised that life offered more.

If I'd once carried out my intentions
I'd leave nothing; a corpse and debris.
And that once I'd pulled on that trigger
The only one hurt would be me.

All at once, I saw that forgiveness
Was not something which others should give.
But that once I had pardoned those others,
I'd be free, with a new life to live.

So at once, I forgave and forgot them.
They're now locked in the back of my head.
And once I did that, I had vision;
Ambition and light up ahead.

We are only once on this planet,
Although sometimes, it can feel like hell,
When you once understand there's a rhythm to life,
There's no reason, on bad times to dwell.

Would we once, recognise which are good times
If everything stayed just the same?
Once we learn to work through the bad times,
Ups and downs become part of the game.

Every once in a while, we are down there.
Before long, we're up on a high.
But once we dwell on the low points
We lose sight of the hills, where we fly.

Once or twice, we will all hit rock bottom,
Though for some, it's hard to break free.
There is always a reason for living,
Just as sunshine and laughter saved me.

The Puzzle

Are we an abnormality
In natures' drive to create
The perfect earthly being
For some distant, future date?

Or are we all individuals
Unique in every way, and
Therefore each a 'perfection',
Whatever others say?

Was I created equal
To others of my kind
Or is that thought simply an illusion
Messing with my mind?

Will we all keep on fighting;
Plundering our planet host;
Arguing over our differences
When we're all similar to most?

Is the jigsaw missing pieces
And when the great gods realise
Should they sweep us back into the box
Ending our 'supreme' rise?

Playtime is Over

The Devil finds work for idle hands
Though 'work' is anathema to rioters and gangs.
They'll find any reason to destroy our lands
While our PC laws bow to all their demands.

But things will not change 'til we've said 'Enough!'
And the police are empowered to start playing rough.
With judges who'll back them with sentences tough.
Then lock them all up; let them know it's no bluff.

Hey, Silent Majority; no longer hide.
We need to be shouting; not hiding inside.
These anarchist 'gangstas' have had a fair ride
But now it is time to lock them inside!

A Sad Farewell

I was reminded, quite recently
Of terms, once heard frequently.
Ones my parents quoted, repeatedly
But seems to have faded, into obscurity.

Now, ignored, with blunt impunity
By the selfish, of our community
When they take, every liberty
As if protected, by immunity.

It's as if, their insecurities
Have warped their personalities
To where those, with these deficiencies
Are lauded, and made celebrities

It's a form of deep insanity
When we allow, bad personality
To practice impropriety
On the rest of our society.

Yes, it's a shame, when there's a tendency
To ignore this loss, complacently.
For, when Respect is in descendency
We wave farewell to Common Decency.

Section 4

Oh, What a Life

Thought for the day.

Never insist that something is foolproof,

because new designs are invented every day

Left or Right

My life once came to a junction
My choices; Left or Right
One looked so straight and easy
The other curved way out of sight.

I had to make a decision
Should I take the easy way out
Or head towards the unknown
By taking the difficult route?

I went for the life of adventure
Hit so many troughs I've lost count
But the heights and peaks I encountered
Taught me; that's what life is about.

If I'd never encountered the bad times
How on earth would I recognise good
And that that which comes to us easily
We appreciate less than we should.

So take a chance in life sometimes
Though the odds may not seem to be good
One never knows what is 'round the bend
But, if you fancy a change, then you should.

Cup of Tea, My Darling?

My wife rolled over and softly said to me
'I love you, my darling, but I want a cup of tea'.
You'll understand, why I didn't dance with glee
Because the digits on the clock said, 'It's half past
three!

But, I hauled my ass out; cracking both my knees
As my only aim in life, is to honour and appease
I live for great moments, just like these
Because I'm married to a woman with a teapot disease.

Now, in my haste, I couldn't find my undies
So, I swiftly donned her thong panties.
Winter- was a'coming, So I started to freeze
As I staggered to the kitchen, threatening to sneeze

No-one was with me but my three puppies
As I went about my business; quite at ease
I bent down to pet them; I love my wee doggies
When suddenly a noise caused my knees to seize

I looked over my shoulder, and what did I see?
Three happy ladies, grinning wide with glee!
Who left the blind up, it surely wasn't me?
But, now I'm in the spotlight - free for all to see.

My ass was up; my bits hung free
While those happy ladies snapped pictures of me
I tried to hide my tackle. I struggled to flee.
But, it was so hard to move, with these damned painful knees.

I'd no time to ponder, as I knew who they'd be
Smokers from the party, next door at number three
I dropped to the floor; and placed the dogs on top of me
As they called to their friends, to share this jamboree

I grabbed onto my tackle, then I killed all the lights
As I pulled down the blinds, so cutting off their sight
But, never again, will I get up in the night
She'll make her own tea now. I'm staying out of sight!

Insomnia

Here we are again, at silly o'clock
Trying not to wake the household up.
Pacing up and down on ice cold boards
Trying to make sense of jumbled words.

Dragged from my bed and guiltless sleep;
Rhythmic words invading too deep.
This cursed ailment has struck yet again
I must jot it down with my pad and pen.

It addles my brain and thins the blood
But, when the words start flowing, they come in a
flood
On these sleepless nights, I have no control
I have to write it down and go with the flow.

I hope Byron woke in the middle of the night;
Sleep-encrusted eyes, in candlelight
Eerily possessed by a ghostly quill
Scratching on dry parchment, against his will.

But I'm just an amateur, so what can I do;
Just a poetic nut with much writing to do?
I sit and scribble, scratching my brain
Too aware that my life is pouring down the drain

But, I can't ignore these moments of 'Zen'
They take me off to worlds way beyond my ken.
I Glance out the window; see the dawning sky;
The world is still asleep, so why aren't I?

Birds are awakening, 'Cheep, cheep, cheep'
But, I'm still denied my rightful sleep.
I grab another breakfast, in a coffee cup
No point going back, so I'm staying up.

So excuse me now, if I'm distracted, when,
I'm not quite there when we meet again.
Only half my brain will be listening to you
The other half is sleeping; it's long overdue!

My Morning Ritual

The calamitous clanger of a cantankerous clock creates immediate contortions that my creaky carcass can hardily cope with.

I stagger, somnolently towards my sanctity of sanitary solitude with sleep sodden eyes, still partly sealed by some, still un-named, sticky substances.

The perfectly positioned peninsular of porcelain pulls me toward it. I plonk my pachyderm posterior, purging pontifically, before peering proudly at the putrid results.

After the ritual of shake, sop and swipe, I stand, shakily, knees screaming silently, before slowly shuffling sideways to the silver-tongued soothsayer standing in the corner - my mirror – before shucking my sleepwear.

I grimace.

Yet again, gallivanting Gremlins have been gracelessly, gambolling overnight. My once graceful, gazelle-like form, glares grouchily, as I gaze at a surprisingly sudden growth in girth.

When did that pendulous, pouch-like package of pork-paunch first appear? Is it trying to protect my once prideful palace of pleasure, or attempting to hide it from even my, once proud peepers?

And behold! Breasts!
Mammalian monstrosities; mounted massively atop once muscled mountains of mean manliness. What merchant of madness made me their misshaped model?

Mmm. Might keep them.

Where, since first shaving, at sweet sixteen, shakily smoothening my sun-kissed skin - should some 'sexy senorita' wish to slaver over it, I now slowly scrape silvered shards of sexless stubble, soon showing the well-earned sentence for an extended existence of sin, supping stupidity, and stepping, senselessly into situations well past my experience and abilities.

That same, gravitous opinion, glares ungraciously from the grim, unforgiving gaze of my grey, red-blotched eyes - a fathomless depth, where only the goading gods of Gomorrah could go.

Ah, the bountiful bonanza of a blameless life!

I blink - slap the teeth in, smile beauteously, then bumble off to another 'brilliant' day.

How was your morning?

On Reflexion

I looked into his bleary eyes;
Saw right through his disguise.
I knew his grim existence
So that is no surprise.

I read his story instantly;
He stared right back at me.
'He's known hell from the inside', I thought
That's plain for all to see.

Those bloodshot orbs bled misery
His wrinkles mapped his life.
His days on earth looked numbered;
Was he soon for the afterlife?

I try an encouraging smile.
A grimace is thrown back.
I wondered, 'Is he worth it?'
But, I didn't turn my back.

I searched his eyes once more;
I inspect every pore,
I decide, 'Maybe, one more day',
And then I slammed the door.

This Demented Writer

There are far too many 'poetries'
Far too many lines
Crashing through my frazzled brain;
Clogging up my mind.

I must stop making notes
It cannot stay this way.
Wide awake, all through the night;
Then a zombie through the day!

There are millions of dead poets
Even more are born each day
I'm trying to be one of them;
But, will I survive the day?

If I have just one good night
I'm sure I will be fine
I'm not even sure this poem is right
Should I try just one more line?

As Long as the Sun Shines

In truth, this retirement is not all it seemed
When, at most, I've achieved just a few of my dreams
And now, as my body falls apart at the seams
There are no re-run vouchers that I can redeem.

As my knees start to scream and my joints all crack;
When every exertion spells an asthma attack
I realise my life has reached a cul-de-sac,
I can only crawl forward; there's no turning back.

When I sit at this window and stare through the glass
There's a pageantry of life, but it drifts slowly past
I know I am grazing on the last of my grass.
The end-days are coming, and they're coming too fast.

The longer I live, the sooner I will die
But, I've lived life to the fullest, so I shouldn't really
cry.
I have family and friends, in contact each day,
And I've all these mental videos; so I often replay.

I may never again share a passionate kiss
Or have glorious hours of hedonistic bliss.
They only come to life as I quietly reminisce.
Who knew that getting old would be anything like
this?

This year is the first time I've really felt cold;
Really chilled to the marrow, I'm growing far too old.
I've played all life's hands; done well, or so I'm told;
And I'm still at the table. I'm not ready to fold.

I've never just sat back, thinking; 'Now it's all too
late'.
I've tried everything once; left scraps upon the plate
If I hadn't even tried, then who could I berate?
To win a one-horse race, one has to leave the gate.

Though I'd love to go back and do it again
I know that most repeats shows are never quite the
same
There's no point lamenting. Though I'm glad to make
the claim;
I did it all; enjoyed it. Now, I'm circling the drain.

So, my frame is now crumbling, in a 'domino effect',
There is too little time, to look back in regret
I may not have achieved much, but what is done is set.
I must believe I did right though, to keep my self-
respect.

I'm at the stairway to heaven, as people may say
But, they've all got it wrong - I'm going the other way.
But, I'm not nearly finished; I'm going out to play.
And as long as the sun shines, I'll have a brilliant day!

Happenchance

There was a late-night knock,
Although, it was no surprise,
The meal I had ordered
Had finally arrived.

The delivery guy looked
Tired and confused.
The bridge he had chosen,
Had long been disused.

But, finally, he'd made it,
Though he'd taken so long,
I told him, 'Come inside'.
He looked so forlorn.

I gave him a drink
Then we shared my meal.
Although a cold stir fry
Was hardly ideal.

We chatted for a while,
Going back through our years,
Until one thing he mentioned
Brought me close to tears.

"I'm an orphan," he said,
 "I've never known my Dad,
And since mom gave me away,
 I have always felt sad."

"I've a brother somewhere.
 I only know his name."
And from that moment onward,
Nothing's been the same.

When he mentioned the name;
Of the brother he had sought,
My heart stopped beating,
And I became distraught.

Because I knew that name;
From many years ago.
But, I wondered, 'Should I tell him?
Does he really need to know?'

You see, we'd served the army;
Been buddies in Iraq.
Until he found an IED
And didn't come back.

"I'm cancerous." He said
"I will not last four weeks."
I knew, right then, what must I do
As tears ran down our cheeks.

So, I decided I would lie.
And said, "Brother, that's my name!"
So now, you all will realise
Why nothing's been the same.

He hugged me very tightly
As he kissed me on both cheeks
And then I ensured his last weeks
Were anything but bleak.

He passed on yesterday, and
While I am very sad
He died with a great big smile on his face -
The brother, I never had.

A Battle With A Bottle

Our life is just one argument
Which I cannot comprehend
I don't know how it started
But it seems to have no end.

We battle every hour
As if we're in a duel
I don't know why I stick with you
I'm a masochistic fool.

But, one day I will pack my bags,
And leave you far behind.
I know the very place to go,
To be with my own kind.

I know you'll try to follow me
But, I will struggle on.
You'll be a tragic memory, when,
The AA makes me strong.

(AA is Alcoholics Anonymous UK
AAA is US version)

My Rise and Fall

I had such great intentions
And even bigger dreams
Though nothing came too easy,
It was harder than it seemed

I worked real hard each day
And plotted through the nights
Trying to make sure
That I did everything right

So, I marched to every order
And danced to every beat.
I knew I should not stand still
I had to move my feet

I had to climb those ladders
High places I would go.
I sharpened both my elbows
And I never once said, 'No'.

I climbed the highest heights
As far as I could see
I met a few glass ceilings, but
They did not obstruct me.

I did so many favours.
I kissed a lot of ass.
I bowed to all my patrons
To ensure they'd let me pass.

But, the shoulders I had stood on
Soon shook and then collapsed.
They swiftly sent me tumbling
Onto my big fat ass

Once I'd slid down to the bottom.
I was told that I should go.
I saw that no-one liked me,
From the highest to the low

It serves me right, they told me,
For reading my own press.
And now I have to start again,
But who can I impress?

Write What You Want

Write what you want.
My bin is right here;
next to my in-tray;
keep sending, I dare.

You might be a banker,
My debtors, or wife.
I'll pay you all sometime
In another life.

But, just you keep chasing.
Keep knocking on that door.
(I no longer live there;
I've moved next door!).

Road to Hell

I'm all alone on my road to hell
With a beaten ol' face and a story to tell,
Of love and hate and joy and pain
No wonder I'm running, running again.
I'm in Hell.

I cheat my women and I steal at cards.
I pick on the weak; fight dirty and hard.
I've met and loved too many to count
But now I'm alone with my future in doubt
And it's Hell.

This ain't no tale to ask for help,
I'm just warning you mothers with young ones to
whelp.
Keep out my way and there's nuthin' to fear.
If you don't listen up; you'll be shedding a tear.
In your Hell.

That ain't no idle, drunken man's threat,
Just don't look this way or you'll soon regret
The day you crossed my demon soul
And joined me in my devil hole,
In Hell.

So, just turn your head and face the sun
Join your friends and have some fun
But, for pity's sake check them carefully
In case one of them is ol' devil me,
From Hell. Your Hell.

Unprepared

(Prior Preparation and Planning
Prevents a Piss Poor Performance).

When I first went back, to advise myself
It didn't go quite as I'd planned.
Though I'd always thought I'd do it one day
I should have prepared beforehand.

As I stood before my younger self
I simply stared right past me
I should've picked a much better time
Because here I was at age three.

So, I tried again for 10 years on
Around the time when I'd had this first thought
But a man of my age would be thrown in a cage
So I ran before I was caught.

But, now that we're here, aged sixty-three
And I know our memories are blurred
How do I tell me, just who I am,
When we cannot recall the code word?

My Last Trip

I'd a psychedelic picture,
Of lullabies and smells,
Of memories, of tastes of love,
In a kaleidoscopic hell.

Black lights were dancing in my head,
The music all misspelt.
My body jerked in spasms
Deaths' fingers coldly felt.

My bowels were loose, my bladder hurt,
My guts a ball of pain.
My arms and legs were liquid fire,
I can't go there again.

I've been on many journeys,
But nothing can eclipse
Those terrifying nightmares
The worst of all my trips.

So I've made a firm decision,
This is not a thing I need
I've left that land to others...
That Wondrous World of Weed!

Section 5

In the Services

Thought for the day.

Betrayal never comes from the enemy.

The Pledge of an Honourable Man

I will fight to my end, to defend: my genes, my kith and kin, my fellow warriors, the innocent, and all who unite with me in the battle against evil and those who would harm or attempt to destroy us.

A Call to Arms

These proud banners of ours, will serve as the rallying
point
for all proud and noble warriors, who stand firm
between
the wicked and the weak.

Many decry its purpose and its righteous cause.
But, they lack the imagination and beliefs which all
good men hold true.

Unity, with good purpose and pure hearts
will always defeat evil, wherever it raises its horned
head.

Gentlemen and Gentlewomen;
Keep your powder dry, your sword close,
and your minds open.

Kill nothing but the enemy.
Take nothing but great care.
Leave nothing but the faint tang of gun smoke
and the corpses of our foe.

Prepare for battle!

At the Bugle Call

Will you sit back, quite contentedly; hands behind your
head,
While the antics of our enemies make everyone see
red?

Do you sleep just like a baby on a warm and cosy
night,
What will it take to make you shout, 'I'm too in this
fight!'?

Are your wrists shackled tightly, behind your cowering
back,
Are you sitting on your hands, too timid to push back?

How far must they go, before you change your mind
Or has your spirit finally retreated? Are you totally
resigned?

If you uncover your ears, will you hear the bugle call?
Or will you refuse to listen, and do nothing at all?

All men of some substance, will stand, true and tall.
No matter their stature, they will answer the call!

In the line of up for battle, where will you stand,
To defend all those you love, and this green and
pleasant land?

Our Guardians

How graceful looks the soldier
As he stands rock-like and still
Belying all those painful hours
On the Parade Ground, learning drill.

How steady are his watchful eyes
As they scan his distant views
Hiding all his inward thoughts
If we only, really knew.

Just look down at his tight, clenched fists
Check the bruises and the cuts
They're not from scrapping in some pub
But from grafting 'til it hurts.

That uniform, so smart and neat
Is more than just for show
The badge upon his headdress
Shows his family, Queen, and Corps.

He swore allegiance to them all
And he'll guard against all foes
Even if it could cost him his life
It's towards the fight he goes.

There are many young folks like him
Who just laugh and run amok
But when danger comes a-knocking
It is he who'll stand and block.

But look a little closer
Is that a young man standing there?
Could it be a well-trained woman
With her bunched-up, well-groomed hair.

They too step forth with courage
To do their bit for us
When it comes down to the wire
They too will fight and cuss.

That's not to say; just soldiers
Are the heroes on our list
Extra-ordinary people
Wear uniforms in our midst.

On the sea, in air, and on the ground
They serve us every day
Like nurses, cops, and fireman
They ensure we'll live today.

So, acknowledge what we owe them
Don't just walk on by
Those folks have sworn an oath to fight
Even if they die.

Running Down The Strand in 1976

'Twas Christmas time in 'Derry town
The season of goodwill.
When normal folks went shopping
And the baddies came to kill.

They hid their nasty firebombs
With timers crudely set
As if more killing might ensure
Their demands would be met.

Headquarters called to warn us,
'Get people off the street!'
Our task: to clear the Strand Road
And start from Clarendon Street.

My buddies ran beside me
You'd think us bulletproof
For we knew there could be gunmen
Who'd be sniping from the roofs.

Civilians ran before us
We herded them like sheep.
We had to get them out there
For now, all life was cheap.

Shop windows blew out left and right
All flames and flying glass
I prayed the next explosion would
Please wait 'til we had passed

We pushed them; screaming, shouting.
Our faces could not show
How bloody scared we were inside,
But none of them would know.

But even then, some turned on us,
Spat, "Leave our kids alone!
We'll never ask for English help.
F##k off. Leave us alone!"

But still, we got them to the end.
Thank God no lives were lost.
But many shops and jobs went up
In this homegrown holocaust.

And now, while many years have passed
Just one thing stays the same.
If it was ever church or politics then,
It's now a criminals domain!

And still they kill and torture
Their neighbours 'cross the street.
But justice comes to all of them,
When their Maker, they do meet.

A Guard of Honour waits for them,
of innocents and Troops,
to bar their way to the Pearly Gates.
They will take the downward route!

Our Hill

The air was so hot, we all began to fry
As the sun blazed down from, that damned empty sky
There was little we could do to dignify,
The sorry-looking state, of every guy.

We'd arrived that morning, before the sun rose high
With a huge pile of ammo and the odd sheet ply
We'd been through a lot, that can't be denied
But to hold this hill, we had to occupy.

We did what we could to fortify,
Using any rocky dips we could modify.
Scraping for shelter and a place to lie.
'til at last we'd created a good place to die.

Finally, time came for some needed shut-eye
As the sun slowly dipped its bright golden eye.
I had just closed my eyes to a quiet lullaby,
When, all of a sudden, came a battle cry.

The enemy were coming; to give us a try.
To force us to leave and wave them, goodbye.
They fired many weapons and let rockets fly.
They lit up the night, like the Fourth of July,

We used all of our weapon in our reply
But, their answer was simply to intensify.
Our ammo ran short, so we cried, 'Resupply!'.
But, things got even scarier, and that is no lie.

They came on like demons, so many, just to died.
But, still, they pressed on. I have no idea why.
We shot them and stabbed them, beneath that
blackening sky
Until, finally, they realised; we would not comply.

They finally gave up, as the new sun rose high.
And, while none of us 'friendlies' had managed to die;
there were so many wounded that we all had to cry.
Their dead in our midst didn't qualify.

I'm not the type of person to speachify,
I've kept this tale short, just to simplify.
That might have been a hill, to the untrained eye
But, that mound, to us, was our Mount Sinai.

To keep it in our hands, many had to die.
We were not there simply to pacify.
And there are no fancy words to beautify;
'A soldiers first duty is to terrify!'

War is up to parliaments to justify;
Then, for the Generals up on high, to stratify
The soldier on the ground will just 'get on by',
'til it's time to go forward, and 'Do or Die.'

The Lonely Warrior

My Brothers and Sister are asleep back there.
I hope they are dreaming; no worries or cares.
For I'll do my duty with honour and flair
Although I'm very tired, I'm fully aware.

My Brothers and Sisters have posted me here.
It's just what I've dreamed of; a warrior career.
So why do I tremble? I'm shaking with fear.
I am sure, as a sentry, I'm well placed out here.

Those Brothers and Sisters, they all have my back.
I know if I call them, they'll soon leave their sacks.
I think I hear movement. Did a twig just crack?
Insurgents are out there. Will they attack?

Please, Brothers and Sisters, hear my quiet prayer.
I'm starting to panic, there's someone out there.
I once had a life without worry or care.
But now I'm involved in this frightening affair.

Oh, Brothers and Sisters, please, where's my relief?
I've been out here too long, that is my belief.
You said just an hour, at my sentry brief
I'm thinking of waving a white handkerchief.

Hey, Brothers and Sisters, please run to my side.
Insurgents are coming, they're creeping inside.
I can't tell their numbers, they're trying to hide.
But, I'll fight them back. I will not let things slide.

Sleep, Brothers and Sisters, please don't hear my
screams.
I think I've just awoken, from a nasty dream.
The sounds that I heard, were not quite what they
seemed,
They come from down there; it's a quiet burbling
stream.

Thanks, Brothers and Sisters, my watch is now o'er,
I've now been relieved and I no longer cower.
My stomach is tight and my mouth is still sour,
But, I'm glad I survived; my very first sentry hour.

The Last Patrol

White-faced, we left the base,
time for one last look around.
But insurgents knew, as they do,
wasn't long 'til we are found.
Soon we take a frag grenade
then RPG's were inward bound.
Men are falling, Corporals calling;
need to cross that open ground.
Legs pumping, hearts thumping;
have to reach the next compound.
Gunships flying, Taliban crying,
multiple rockets all hell-bound.
Mortars popping, more men dropping,
body parts are all around.
Bodies flying, people dying,
screaming wounded; terrible sounds.
Then cross a ditch, where life's a bitch,
it's hand to hand; the victor crowned.
More men bleeding, wounded pleading,
thank God none make English sounds.

Then we see escapees flee; running,
scampering, scared foxhounds.
But life's unfair; we call in air
and bomb them where they've run to ground.
We count our men. A quick amen,
no time for speeches; too profound.
So it's sort our heads as we count the dead,
and get our wounded safety bound.
But soon we hear what soldiers fear,
artillery shells are inward-bound.
The leaders shout, "Move on out,
this is no longer our playground".
We dash out fast, before first blast,
and still, none of us earns a Reaper Shroud.
Then when we ask, for our next task,
Head Quarters has us all spellbound.
For all you hear, is one great cheer,
even now the echoes still resound.
"Get back to base, and pack your case,
your job is done, you're homeward-bound!"

Tour over!

.

At The Cenotaph

I wonder if I'm worthy,
As I stand, saluting you.
Though we wore a similar uniform,
I'd never measure up to you.

I'm a simple man, who served his land,
As you did, way back then
But, while I have now retired in life,
You didn't come back again.

I followed in your footsteps
'Though with no real sacrifice;
But, while I too served with honour,
You paid the ultimate price.

Many millions lost their lives through strife
Too many; maimed and hurt.
Now poppy fields remind us of
Those who lie beneath the dirt.

But, your hopes and dreams weren't wasted
Your lives weren't lost for naught
The reasons I can stand here now
Are the freedoms your lives bought.

So, I hang my head to honour you
While my spine is stiff with pride
Because folks like you ensured; England
Was never occupied.

Our Sentinels

For countless years men have stood right there;
Guardians of this land.
Tho' weapons changed throughout the years
They've defended this foreland.

Whether they came from north, east, or south
From the west, from skies or sea
These fighting men – Great British Men
Still fought to keep us free.

Their earthly bodies; long since dust
Their courage reminds us all;
With that fighting spirit of our uniformed men
Britain will never fall!

Section 5

The Dark Side of Life.

Fair Warning!

This section contains poems addressing Illness, Death, and Grief.
Please, don't be upset by its content.

Thought for the day.

The journey of life is rocky
and the only way around is through.

Foreword to
His Final Parade

Norse mythology has it that half of all warriors who died in battle went to Valhalla (The Hall of the Slain) – an enormous, majestic hall located in Asgard - to serve Odin, and to drink and make merry until the next battle.

The other half went to Folkvangr (The Army Field) to serve his wife, the goddess Freyja, in a similar manner.

Today, soldiers of the British Army speak of their own version of Valhalla.

We call it '**The Squadron Bar**'.

His Final Parade

We lost another good brother today
Nor from a bullet, or someone we could slay.
An insidious enemy crept in one day,
Then schemed in the shadows to take him away.

That lingering passing; the one we all dread;
Ignores all our hopes to die quickly in bed.
It spread through his body; invaded his head
He fought a good battle, but still, he lies dead.

Now we're standing here, erect, with heads bowed
Though shattered in grief, we're far from being cowed
While our friend has now parted, away from this crowd
We salute you, our brother; you did us all proud.

Although he has now left, he has not gone far
He's here in our hearts; in our lifes' memoir
But we'll follow on, in times not too far
Then, we will all meet again, in The Squadron Bar.

Then we'll raise our glasses, to the ones we have left
To the ones who are grieving; the ones now bereft
But, for now, we raise ours, to one of the best:
Farewell, our dear Brother, it's your time to rest.

Grief Is But Love

When we've just lost a partner, a friend, or a beau
We're faced with a void, like a physical blow;
While our tears and our cries will outwardly show;
What's torn from your hearts, only we know.

Yet, there are some who will push us to, 'live on', and grow.
To, 'get over' our grief, and get on with the show.
May they never know, why 'healing' is so slow,
and that, grief is but love, with nowhere to go.

This, I Know

I have no voice,
Though I'm far from dead
No-one can hear
The screams in my head
I just lie here, silently,
Staring ahead
Surrounded by strangers;
Crowding my bed.

They seem to take turns;
Changing guard by the day
And it disturbs me some,
When they kneel down and pray.
They all think I'm deaf,
But I hear all they say
Though they don't talk to me;
I'm just here, on display.

I've been searching my head,
Hoping something might show
A return of my memory,
But the going is slow.
Still, there is one small thing;
That I'm very pleased to know:
I've just heard a young nurse say;
My name is John Doe.

A Friend Suffers

I'm sitting here alone
at very dark o'clock
Eating bloody Happy Meals
Although my heart's a rock

Not knowing how my friend feels now
Just sends my mind amok
Whose god created Parkinson's?
What a way to treat his flock!

My friend lives many miles away
We chat by internet
He's undergoing treatments
And he knows how rough it gets.

I wish I had a magic wand -
How foolish can I get?
There's not a thing that I can do
But suck this cigarette!

I'm feeling pretty useless.
I need to be alone.
There are far too many night owls here,
With worries of their own
.

I know I should just walk on out;
This place I should disown
But misery seeks company,
And here we've found a home.

So, I'll just sit here for a little while
And then be on my way
I've said my prayers and had a curse
So, there's nothing more to say.

If prayer counts for anything
His disease will go away.
But if life has taught me anything
It's just another crappy day!

Waves Upon the Sand

We can't keep a wave upon the sand
Nor hold rainbows in our outstretched hands.
It makes no difference where we stand
When a loved one passes to their promised land

We may curse and swear; even pray to our gods
But all our wishes are futile words.
We must accept; life is short and flawed
Then smile at their memories; cry and applaud.

A Ray of Hope

I know you live in Paradise
Of this, I'm quite convinced
I search each night the darkened skies
For just one fleeting glimpse

Until we meet, I'm all alone
Surrounded by my pain
As you drift through the heavens
I pray; we'll meet again.

That Place Called Depression

I have been to that place called depression,
It's down there 'twix dread and despair.
I'll try very hard to describe it to you,
And the possible way out of there.

It's a Hell of a place made of boxes and cells.
No windows. No lights and no doors.
Though how you arrived is an unconscious dive.
Stay too long and you'll sink through the floor.

The unlimited depth a depression can get
Seems unending, but can be repaired.
Though, it will never go right if you give up the fight,
And allow it a one-way affair.

Now, the levels above are the place you should be.
While below, is a life full of dread.
From that place you must see, there's a way to break free.
You can leave there by using your head.

You must find that faint glimmer of hope in your heart.
Look inside, you will find its dim spark.
It's that, which will get you out of that place
And assist you to push back the dark.

When you find it, just fan it 'til it starts to glow.
Then you'll see to the left and the right.
But the only way out of that desolate place,
Is to stand up and head for the light.

The light is above you, the ceiling is frail,
It just needs the strength of your will.
But, if it's too hard to climb out on your own,
Ask for help, take a hand; let them pull.

That Place Called Depression
(Short Version)

I have been to that place called depression,
It's down there 'twixt dread and despair.
I do find it hard to describe it to you,
But, please don't make plans to go there.

But, if you do find you're heading that way,
Don't look down, don't look left, don't look right,
For the only way out of that desolate place
Is to stand up and head for the light.

The light is above you, the ceiling is frail,
You must use the strength of your will,
But if it's too hard to climb out on your own,
We are here. Take our hands. Let us pull.

Seeking

Early morning, clearing skies
Rest on a glistening dew
Though, if I could see ten thousand miles
I know I'd not see you.

Our glory days are bright and clear
Throughout my dreams of you
Your warmth, your touch, remembered in
The life I shared with you.

At night I dream of happiness,
But, at dawn, they're cast askew
When the morning sun reminds me
Of the day when I lost you.

So, every day I'll stumble on;
My search for you renewed
No matter what the daylight says say
Some day, I will join you.

Our Angel Born Sleeping

Will someone hear our silent scream
And awake us from this dreadful dream
Then tell us that it's all untrue;
That this poor baby did pull through?

Then say, "He lived. He did not die.
He took a breath; let out a cry".
But no-one can. Life's so unfair,
He died pre-birth; no smiles to share.

Many emotions have run wild,
At the loss of this gorgeous, cherished child.
There's been anger, guilt, confusion, fear.
At the injustice done to this child here.

No, we'll never hear his laughs, his cries,
His fantasies or little white lies.
He'll have no falls, no fears, no tears;
Nor great concerns in future years.

But there is one good thing
I can say to you all;
He knew the greatest gift of all,
LOVE from family, and friends, such as we.

From his time of conception,
He's felt love and affection
Through the time he was carried,
All these months, to perfection,
Yes, he knew the loveliest feeling of all,
That of being loved!

So dry those sad tears,
and allay all your fear.
He'll live on, in our hearts, for many a year.

And when the dark times come,
With grief freezing you numb,
Please try to recall, the feeling that's here.
It's love.

Though he's not ours for keeping,
It's time to stop weeping.
s we smile on this child;
Our Angel Born Sleeping.

His Last Words

He lay there, near exhaustion
The end was now drawing near
There was so much he'd left unsaid
To his love of all these years

He confessed all his secrets;
While reliving all his fears
His voice, so often faltering
Often sounding quite unclear.

They pressed their lips together
As they shared hot salty tears
Then he whispered his last words,
'I must leave you now, my dear.'

Live On

All things end
I must ascend
I've lingered long
I can't carry on.

My time has come
I can hear the drum
Sweet angels sing
To guide me

But, if I'm in your mind
You're not left behind
I have not gone far;
I've just travelled on.

If I'm in your heart
We are apart
Our love is strong
So you may journey on.

                    Live on.

Let Go

If you've nursed a bird with a broken wing,
Or comforted a friend as they were crying.
If you've supported a cause until you were done,
Or raised a child until they could run

Then the hardest part, as you will know,
Is the simple act of letting go.
Of knowing that your job is done,
And it's time for them to fly or run.

But as hard as it is, you must agree,
We did it all to set them free:
To release our bond of loving care,
To throw that bird into the air,

Or push that child as far as can be
And then turn our backs so they cannot see
Our tears of love-joy-pain and sadness,
As they take their place in this world of madness.

Let go.
Let go.
Let go.

Pictures of You

Though you passed so long ago
My darling, I still miss you so.

Your voice; still clearly heard;
Sad emotions, so easily stirred

But still, I can shuffle through
These mental pictures of you

And while they are in my head
And you have gone ahead

I feel you, right by my side
Knowing; I'm not far behind.

Section 6

Nature Has The Last Word

Thought for the day

Because of the light of the moon,
Silver is found on the moor,
And because of the light of the sun,
There is gold on the walls of the poor.
Because of the light of the stars,
Planets are found in the stream,
(And because of the light in your eyes
There is love in the depth of my dream).

Poem by Francis Carling

A Fluttering of Sleet

Up-turned cars and
Abandoned heaps
Call out the snowploughs
It's millimetres deep!

Schools close down
Hear the parents bleat
What to do with children;
Instagram or Tweet.

Once again the newshounds
Stamp their feet
Pointing out the obvious
Isn't that sweet?

The seasons come
And the seasons go
But, this is down to Brexit
Didn't you know?

The Silent Intruder

Into the darkness, in the dark, cold night
Sneaks our protagonist, eyes steely bright

Into our gardens, he silently creeps
Casing the town as everyone sleeps

Over our rooftops, and down every road
He slithers around like a slimy toad

Into the valleys and over the hills
If we're caught unwary, he often kills

When children awake, they all think it's fun
To play with him in the winter sun

But please be aware, he doesn't play nice
Because Jack Frost bites, and he won't think twice!

As Winter Falls to Springtime

As winter falls to Springtime
The battle nearly won
When daffodils rise from the ground
Resurgence has begun

At early morning sunrise
Darkness runs to hide
Returning starlings swoop from high
As children run outside

Our nightmares fade from memory
As light overcomes the gloom
The human race once more will march
From quilted catacombs.

A warming sun brings longer days
Heads lift with lengthening strides
And lovers meet their brides to be
As Cupids arrows fly

Moments in Time

As winter trades with springtime
And summer fades to fall
Is it moments, or a season
You will think is best of all?

As the day before tomorrow
Fades, to be yesterday
What will you remember
At the closing of the day?

While seconds mark our heartbeats;
And our lives are measured in years
How will you be remembered
When discussed amongst your peers?

(And as time marches on, regardless;
When all thing die, as they must
Will the earth miss a single heartbeat
When the human race is dust?)

The Regal Robin Red-Breast

Our tiny survivor of winters bleak
Ruby red breast and proud physique
Traps his catch in his pointed beak
This flycatcher of ancient mystique.

Singing loudly, his ribald song
His bouncing dance keeps us all in thrall
Erithacus rubecula, so regal; so small
It's a wonder he survives at all.

The King is Dead.
Long Live the Queen

When old Saint Steven hid in his tree
King Wren, sang loudly, proud and free

But that ribald singing soon told them all
Where Steven hid; it was a bitter wrawl.

Wild boys threw stones at the King Wrens' head
And now, like Steven, King Wren is dead.

Though she took his death the worse of all
Queen Wren refused a widows shawl

Though she uses her new titled name
Queen Jeni-Wren continues to reign

And even though there is only she
The whole world bows on bended knee

Though Queen Jeni-Wren was born to reign
Men don't honour her quite the same

Because old Steven died that day
Boxing Day is Saint Stevens Day.

Jack the Thief

Jack the robber. Jack the thief
Skimming skies; causing grief
Anything shiny; a glittering gem
Never to be seen by the owner again.

Jack on the prowl across our roofs
Acting so cool. He's so aloof.
Afraid of nothing; giving it large
Informing the world that he's in charge

Jack in uniform – grey and black
With a jet black mask and silver scarf.
Any challenge is such a joke
Jack even laughs at human folk

Jack knows his rights under the law;
Though day by day, he breaks them all
Some have a license, shoot him down
But, who could kill that crazy old clown?

No Hiding Place

I thought I'd be well hidden,
Were no-one else could see.
But, I still felt many eyeballs
Were looking right at me.

I feared an army marching
Then creeping up on me
Or parachutes descending
As silent as can be.

I looked around - saw nothing.
But how wrong could I be?
They came from all directions;
They were in the god-damned tree!

Bloody caterpillars!

Cat Burglar.

I peeked through every window;
Then, I saw her laying there
Her fur-lined nest was obvious
I couldn't help but stare.

I thought my heart belonged with her,
In warmth I longed to share;
Although this window was ajar,
I knew I shouldn't dare.

But still, she was so beautiful;
Completely unaware.
I could not leave that vision
She was the answer to my prayer.

I hopped onto the windowsill;
Stepped quietly to a chair
I'd hoped to move in quietly
But I gave her such a scare.

All at once, she started screaming
It was my fault, to be fair.
She's obviously not a cat fan
So, I ran the hell out of there!

A Taste for Honey

A beautiful lady
once said to me
You may taste my honey,
when I'm the Queen Bee

And ever since then,
 I've sat by her tree
Waiting for Honey
to come down to me

But each day I wait
what do I see
Thousands of suitors
flying past me

There's a buzz in the air
They're eating for free
No-one listens
to my heartfelt pleas

Soon none will be left
for a cur like me
Oh, how I wish
I'd been born a bee.

Natures Wrath

It was an awesome night of wonder
Lightening speared torrential skies
The atmosphere boomed with thunder
Each flash; a total surprise

We held our ears, defenceless
Though closed, our eyes couldn't cope
The cacophony continued relentless
All senses a kaleidoscope

But still we lay there beneath it
Forcing breath into aching lungs
In wonder at natures wild spirit
As it spat out its rage in forked tongues.

About the Author

Born in the Scottish borderlands town of Kelso in 1950; reared and Secondary School educated the then steelworks town, of Corby, Northamptonshire in England.

He left school without gaining any formal qualifications.

He married his childhood sweetheart in 1968, before enlisting in the British Corps of Royal Engineers in 1971 – a career that lasted 22 years.

In his working life, he has become the 'Jack of all trades, but master of none' in many artisan, skilled and non-skilled disciplines, ranging from: catering and construction, through to salesmanship, management, and running his own transport business.

He took up poetry writing as a hobby during his early retirement years in Turkey.

In 2021, he and his wife celebrate their 53rd wedding anniversary, along with their two children, five grandchildren, and, at the time of writing, one great-grandson.

He now lives, contentedly, with family close at hand in Dover, England

April 2021

Printed in Great Britain
by Amazon